easy cookies

easy cookies

Linda Collister

photography by Diana Miller

RYLAND
PETERS
& SMALL

LONDON NEW YORK

First published in Great Britain in 2005
by Ryland Peters & Small
20–21 Jockey's Fields
London WC1R 4BW
www.rylandpeters.com

10 9 8 7 6 5 4 3 2 1

Printed in China

ISBN 1 84172 951 5

A CIP record for this book is available
from the British Library.

Dedication
To Emily, Daniel and Stevie.

Acknowledgements
I would to thank the many people who
helped with this book; Elsa Petersen-
Schepelern, Steve Painter, Diana Miller,
Róisín Nield, Barbara Levy, Simon
Silverwood and Alan Hertz.

Senior Designer Steve Painter
Commissioning Editor
   Elsa Petersen-Schepelern
Production Patricia Harrington
Art Director Gabriella Le Grazie
Publishing Director Alison Starling

Food Stylist Linda Collister
Prop Stylist Róisín Nield

Notes
• All spoon measurements are level
unless otherwise specified.
• All eggs are large unless otherwise
specified.
• Before baking, weigh or measure all
ingredients exactly and prepare baking
sheets.
• Ovens should be preheated to the
specified temperature. Recipes in this
book were tested in several kinds of
oven – all work slightly differently.
I recommend using an oven thermometer
and consulting the maker's handbook for
special instructions.

contents

introduction

Few of us can resist a cookie warm from the oven; add a glass of milk or a cup of coffee or tea and you have pure, simple pleasure.

Since you can't make just one, and you really shouldn't eat the whole batch yourself, home-baked cookies are ideal for sharing. They are adaptable, too: luckily there is no 'proper' time of day to eat a cookie, no rules that say you can't eat cheese crackers with soup or chocolate biscuits with ice cream.

The other delight of cookies is their simplicity: few ingredients, easy assembly and rapid baking. The key to success is good materials like unsalted butter, free-range eggs, golden caster sugar, fresh flour. Buy organic if you can. For some recipes the eggs and butter should be used at room temperature rather than straight from the refrigerator.

Nuts and chocolate are key ingredients for many recipes; the flavour of the final result will depend on their quality. Nuts go rancid very quickly, so buy in small quantities and use a fresh packet (after opening, wrap the rest of the packet tightly and store in the freezer). Buy the best chocolate you can afford – these days there is a good range at most supermarkets (even excellent Fairtrade chocolate). It's worth trying out a few small bars to find the one you really enjoy.

These biscuits and cookies are easy to prepare, but for some recipes an electric mixer or food processor will speed up the beating, mixing or chopping.

Other equipment is quite basic, but a good, heavy-duty baking tray is invaluable. I've been using mine on an almost daily basis for 20 years, so it has repaid the initial investment. My son now wants one of his own. A large wire cooling rack is very convenient, though you can also use the rack from the grill pan or an oven shelf. An airtight container for storing your cookies will also come in handy, while many cookies and biscuits can be frozen.

You also need a good, controllable oven. It is worth getting an inexpensive oven thermometer to double-check the temperature, plus a kitchen timer: thermostats and clocks, even on the best of ovens, can be unreliable. The cooking times are guidelines; your oven handbook and your own oven knowledge will teach you which shelf works best, and baking times should be reduced for fan ovens.

In this book, you'll find all sorts of cookies, biscuits and crackers – the chunky All-American; the thin and crispy Continental; the rich, buttery Scottish shortbread. I can't ever decide on a favourite; it all depends on the weather.

classics

These cookies are always popular, whether plain or flavoured with dried fruit or spices. Use old-fashioned porridge oats or rolled oats rather than 'instant'.

classic oat cookies

115 g unsalted butter, very soft

140 g light muscovado sugar

1 large egg, beaten

1 tablespoon milk

½ teaspoon vanilla essence

100 g self-raising flour

150 g porridge oats

several baking trays, very lightly greased

Makes 24

Put the butter, sugar, egg, milk and vanilla in a bowl and beat well using an electric mixer or whisk, or a wooden spoon. Add the flour and oats and mix well with the wooden spoon.

Put heaped teaspoons of dough onto the prepared baking trays, spacing them well apart.

Bake in a preheated oven at 180°C (350°F) Gas 4 for 12–15 minutes until lightly browned around the edges.

Let cool on the trays for 2 minutes, then transfer to a wire rack to cool completely.

Store in an airtight container and eat within 5 days or freeze for up to a month.

Variations At the same time as the flour, add either:
• 75 g dried fruit (raisins, cherries, cranberries or blueberries)
• 1 teaspoon ground cinnamon, 1 teaspoon mixed spice and 2 pinches of ground black pepper
• 60 g choc chips and 25 g shredded or chopped almonds.

For the best flavour, use a good-quality peanut butter with no added sugar. The crunchy coating is made by rolling the cookie mixture in roasted (but unsalted) peanuts before baking.

extra-crunchy peanut butter cookies

115 g unsalted butter, softened

125 g crunchy peanut butter

140 g light muscovado sugar

1 large egg, lightly beaten

½ teaspoon vanilla essence

225 g self-raising flour

200 g roasted unsalted peanut halves

several baking trays, greased

Makes 20

Put the soft butter, peanut butter, sugar, beaten egg, vanilla and flour in a large bowl. Mix well with a wooden spoon. When thoroughly combined, take walnut-sized portions of the dough (about a tablespoon) and roll into balls with your hands. Put the peanut halves in a shallow dish, then roll the dough in the nuts. Arrange the balls well apart on the prepared trays, then gently flatten slightly with your fingers.

Bake in a preheated oven at 180°C (350 F) Gas 4 for 12–15 minutes until light golden brown.

Let cool on the trays for a couple of minutes to firm up, then transfer to a wire rack to cool completely.

Store in an airtight container and eat within 5 days or freeze for up to a month.

The classic recipe is three parts flour, two parts butter and one part sugar, with some of the flour replaced with rice flour, ground rice or cornflour to give the traditional light, short and sandy texture. The better the butter you use, the finer the flavour and texture – a well-salted, cheap, blended butter will make the shortbread heavier. Shortbread can be thinly rolled and cut into discs, or pressed into a shallow cake tin to make the usual thicker 'petticoat tails'.

scottish shortbread

260 g plain flour

40 g rice flour, ground rice or cornflour

100 g caster sugar, plus a little extra for sprinkling

200 g unsalted butter, chilled and diced

a sandwich tin, about 23 cm diameter, lightly greased

or a 7.5 cm fluted round biscuit cutter and several baking trays, greased

Makes about 20 rounds or 12 petticoat tails

Put the plain flour, rice flour (or ground rice, or cornflour) and sugar in a food processor. Process until thoroughly mixed. Add the diced butter and process until the ingredients come together to make a ball of dough. Carefully remove the dough from the machine.

If making petticoat tails, lightly flour your fingers, then gently press the dough into the cake tin to make an even layer. Prick the dough all over with a fork, then gently score into 12 segments or wedges using a sharp, pointed knife.

If making thin rounds, roll out the dough on a lightly floured work surface with a floured rolling pin to about 5 mm thick and cut out rounds with the biscuit cutter. Gently knead the trimmings, then re-roll and cut out more rounds. Put the rounds slightly apart on the prepared baking trays. Prick with a fork.

Chill the shortbread for 15 minutes, then bake in a preheated oven at 180°C (350°F) Gas 4 for 15–20 minutes for the petticoat tails and 10–12 minutes for the rounds, until just firm and barely coloured. Sprinkle the shortbread with a little sugar, then let cool for 2 minutes.

For petticoat tails, cut the segments along the marked lines, then leave until cold before removing from the tin. For the rounds, transfer to a wire rack to cool completely.

Store in an airtight container and eat within a week or freeze for up to a month.

I've been eating and making these cookies since
I could walk. The recipe comes from my grandmother,
and is now a favourite with a fourth generation.

gingerbread cookies

350 g self-raising flour

a pinch of salt

200 g golden caster sugar,
plus extra for sprinkling

2 teaspoons ground ginger

2 teaspoons ground cinnamon

1 teaspoon bicarbonate of soda

115 g unsalted butter

85 g black treacle

1 large egg, beaten

several baking trays, greased

Makes 30

Sift the flour, salt, sugar, ginger, cinnamon and bicarbonate of soda into a large bowl. Heat the butter and black treacle very gently in a small saucepan until melted.

Pour onto the dry ingredients, add the beaten egg and mix thoroughly with a wooden spoon. Using your hands, roll the dough into 30 walnut-sized balls. Arrange well apart on the prepared trays, then flatten slightly with your fingers. Sprinkle with a little sugar, then bake in a preheated oven at 160°C (325°F) Gas 3 for 12–15 minutes or until firm and lightly browned. Remove from the oven and let cool on the trays for 2 minutes. Transfer to a wire rack to cool completely.

Store in an airtight container and eat within 5 days or freeze for up to a month.

Variation To make Stem Ginger Biscuits, replace the treacle with golden syrup. Finely chop 2 pieces (40 g) of stem ginger in syrup (drained) and add with the egg.

Parkin is a kind of sticky gingerbread from Yorkshire, made with oatmeal, black treacle and spice. These cookies are made from the same ingredients and have the same flavour and a crunchy texture.

parkin cookies

115 g self-raising flour

115 g fine oatmeal

1 teaspoon ground ginger

½ teaspoon ground allspice

3 tablespoons dark muscovado sugar

85 g unsalted butter

2 tablespoons golden syrup

1 tablespoon black treacle

icing sugar, for dusting (optional)

several baking trays, greased

Makes 20

Put the flour, oatmeal, ginger, allspice and sugar in a large bowl and mix well. Make a hollow in the centre.

Put the butter, golden syrup and treacle in a small saucepan and heat gently until melted.

Pour the mixture into the hollow in the dry ingredients and mix well with a wooden spoon. Using floured hands, take walnut-sized portions of the dough (about a tablespoon) and roll into balls. Set well apart on the prepared trays. Bake in a preheated oven at 180°C (350°F) Gas 4 for 15 minutes until firm.

Let cool on the trays for 2 minutes to firm up, then transfer to a wire rack to cool completely. Serve dusted with icing sugar, if using.

Store in an airtight container and eat within 5 days or freeze for up to a month.

The rich, soft dough should be thoroughly chilled before being sliced and baked. The dough can be stored in the refrigerator for up to a week, or frozen for up to a month before finishing the recipe. The result is a melt-in-the-mouth cookie.

ice-box cookies

200 g unsalted butter, at room temperature

100 g icing sugar, sifted

1 teaspoon real vanilla essence

80 g porridge oats

½ teaspoon baking powder

225 g plain flour

caster sugar, for sprinkling

several baking trays, greased

Makes about 18

Put the soft butter and icing sugar in a large bowl and beat with a wooden spoon or electric mixer (or whisk) on low speed, until light and fluffy. Beat in the vanilla, then stir in the oats.

Sieve the baking powder and flour into the bowl, then mix with your hands or a wooden spoon to make a slightly soft but not sticky dough.

Shape the dough into a log about 7 cm diameter, then wrap thoroughly in clingfilm or greaseproof paper. Chill until firm – at least 30 minutes or up to a week. The dough can be frozen for up to a month, then defrosted in the refrigerator for 12 hours.

Slice the log into rounds about 5 mm thick, then arrange slightly apart on the prepared baking trays. Sprinkle lightly with the sugar.

Bake in a preheated oven at 160°C (325°F) Gas 3 for 15–20 minutes until lightly golden around the edges.

Let cool on the tray for 2 minutes, then transfer to a wire rack to cool completely.

Store in an airtight container and eat within 5 days or freeze for up to a month.

Variation Before baking, sprinkle the top of each cookie with chocolate chips or pieces (about 50 g) or with grated plain chocolate (about 40 g).

For a real taste of Normandy, use their delicious unsalted butter. The dough is made in a processor, then rolled out and cut into pretty fluted discs or shaped into a log and sliced into rounds. The tops of the cookies are brushed with egg to give a rich, glossy finish, then patterned with a fork.

french sablés

200 g plain flour

a pinch of salt

80 g icing sugar

130 g unsalted butter, chilled and diced

3 large egg yolks

½ teaspoon real vanilla essence

1 egg, beaten, to glaze

a fluted biscuit cutter, 9 cm diameter

several baking trays, greased

Makes about 10

Put the flour, salt, sugar and diced butter in a food processor. Process until the mixture looks like fine crumbs. Add the egg yolks and vanilla and process again until the mixture comes together to make a firm dough. Remove from the processor.

To make the rolled out cookies, wrap the dough well in clingfilm, then chill for 30 minutes or until firm. Roll out the chilled dough on a lightly floured work surface to about 5 mm thick. Cut out rounds with the fluted cutter and arrange them slightly apart on the prepared trays. Knead the trimmings together, roll again and cut out more rounds.

To make sliced cookies, shape the dough into a log about 6 x 8 cm. Wrap and chill for 1 hour or until very firm. The dough can be kept in the refrigerator for up to 2 days. Using a large, sharp knife, slice the dough into rounds about 5 mm thick and arrange them slightly apart on the prepared trays, 4–5 on each pan.

Brush the rounds very lightly with beaten egg, then chill for 15 minutes.

Brush again with beaten egg, prick all over with a fork, then mark with the prongs to make a neat pattern.

Bake in a preheated oven at 180°C (350°F) Gas 4 for 12–15 minutes or until a good golden brown.

Let cool on the trays for 2 minutes, then transfer to a wire rack to cool completely. Store in an airtight container and eat within a week or freeze for up to a month.

chocolate

Always popular and hard to beat! I've adapted the classic recipe so that it uses less sugar and more nuts. Use plain chocolate broken up into chunks or a bag of choc chips.

classic choc chip cookies

175 g self-raising flour

a pinch of salt

a good pinch of bicarbonate of soda

115 g unsalted butter, very soft

60 g caster sugar

60 g light muscovado sugar

½ teaspoon real vanilla essence

1 large egg, lightly beaten

175 g plain choc chunks or chips

75 g walnut or pecan pieces

several baking trays, greased

Makes 24

Put all the ingredients in a large bowl and mix thoroughly with a wooden spoon.

Drop heaped teaspoons of the mixture onto the prepared trays, spacing them well apart.

Bake in a preheated oven at 190°C (375°F) Gas 5 for 8–10 minutes until lightly coloured and just firm.

Let cool on the trays for a minute, then transfer to a wire rack to cool completely.

Store in an airtight container and eat within 5 days or freeze for up to a month.

The original mocha was a fine Arabian coffee shipped from a port in Yemen called Mocha. Now the word means either a hot drink made of coffee and chocolate together, or other sweet mixtures using these two flavours. These little cookies are perfect with a cup of coffee after dinner.

mocha kisses

180 g self-raising flour

90 g caster sugar

90 g unsalted butter, chilled and cut into small pieces

2 teaspoons instant coffee granules or powder

1 large egg

Filling

75 g unsalted butter, very soft

150 g icing sugar

2 teaspoons instant coffee granules or powder

2 teaspoons cocoa powder

several baking trays, greased

Makes 9

If making the dough by hand, mix the flour and sugar in a bowl. Add the pieces of butter and, using the tips of your fingers, rub in until the mixture looks like breadcrumbs. Put the coffee in a bowl and dissolve in 1 teaspoon of warm water. Add the egg and beat lightly. Stir the egg and coffee mixture into the flour mixture with a wooden spoon. Mix well so that the ingredients come together to make a firm dough.

Alternatively, put the flour, sugar and pieces of butter in a food processor. Process until the mixture looks like breadcrumbs. Add the egg, then the coffee dissolved in a teaspoon of warm water. Process until the dough comes together. Carefully remove from the machine.

Flour your hands and roll the dough into 18 walnut-sized balls. Arrange them slightly apart on the prepared baking trays and bake in a preheated oven at 160°C (325°F) Gas 3 for 10–15 minutes until a light golden colour.

Remove from the oven, let cool on the tray for 2 minutes, then transfer to a wire rack to cool completely.

Meanwhile, to make the filling, put the soft butter, sugar, coffee and cocoa in a bowl and beat well with a wooden spoon or electric mixer or whisk – there will be flecks of coffee in the smooth icing. Use to sandwich the cookies in pairs.

Store in an airtight container and eat within 24 hours. Not suitable for freezing.

Variation To make Coffee Walnut Kisses, make the filling without the cocoa. Stir in 3 tablespoons chopped walnuts and use the crunchy coffee walnut icing to sandwich the cookies.

Good quality plain chocolate is mixed into these cookies as chunks and as a powder (by simply processing with the flour).

double chocolate pecans

100 g porridge oats or rolled oats (not instant)

140 g plain flour

½ teaspoon baking powder

½ teaspoon bicarbonate of soda

85 g light muscovado sugar

200 g plain chocolate, broken up

115 g unsalted butter, very soft

1 large egg, beaten

100 g pecan pieces

several baking trays, greased

Makes 24

Put the oats in a food processor. Add the flour, baking powder, bicarbonate of soda, the sugar and half of the chocolate pieces. Process until the mixture has a sandy texture.

Put the soft butter, beaten egg, pecan pieces and the remaining pieces of chocolate in a large bowl. Add the mixture from the processor and mix well with a wooden spoon or your hands to make a firm dough.

Roll walnut-sized pieces of dough into balls using your hands. Arrange well apart on the prepared baking trays and flatten slightly with the back of a fork. Bake in a preheated oven at 190°C (375°F) Gas 5 for 12–15 minutes until almost firm.

Let cool on the trays for 2 minutes, then transfer to a wire rack to cool completely.

Store in an airtight container and eat within 5 days or freeze for up to a month.

A simple melt-and-mix recipe, best made with very good plain chocolate – no baking needed. The result is a really rich chocolate biscuit, ideal with coffee after a meal.

chilled chocolate biscuits

125 g unsalted butter

3 tablespoons golden syrup

200 g good quality plain chocolate, broken up

60 g nuts (whole almonds, hazelnuts, walnuts or a mixture)

30 g dried cherries or cranberries

60 g raisins

100 g digestive biscuits or plain crisp biscuits such as Petit Beurre

a Swiss roll tin or shallow baking tin about 30 x 20 cm, base-lined with non-stick baking parchment

Makes 24

Put the butter, syrup and chocolate in a heatproof bowl. Set the bowl over a saucepan of gently simmering water and melt gently, stirring frequently.

Remove the bowl from the pan and add the whole nuts, cherries and raisins.

Break up the biscuits into pieces the size of your thumbnail and add to the bowl. Mix gently with a wooden spoon.

When thoroughly mixed, transfer to the prepared tin and spread evenly. Chill until firm, about 2 hours.

Cut into 24 squares and remove from the tin. Serve chilled. Store in the refrigerator in an airtight container for up to a week.

Variations
- For the holidays, soak the raisins in 2 tablespoons brandy for 1–2 hours before using.
- For children, replace the dried cherries with mini marshmallows.

A very quick, rich recipe using plain chocolate and a food processor. Good served with ice cream.

chocolate fudge cookies

75 g caster sugar

75 g light muscovado sugar

140 g good plain chocolate, broken up

110 g unsalted butter, chilled and diced

150 g plain flour

½ teaspoon baking powder

1 large egg, lightly beaten

several baking trays, greased

Makes about 20

Put both the sugars in a food processor. Add the pieces of chocolate, then process until the mixture has a sandy texture.

Add the pieces of butter, flour, baking powder and egg and process until the mixture comes together to make a firm dough. Carefully remove from the machine.

Lightly flour your hands and roll the dough into about 20 walnut-sized balls. Arrange them, spaced well apart, on the prepared trays.

Bake in a preheated oven at 180°C (350°F) Gas 4 for 12–15 minutes until firm.

Let cool on the trays for 2 minutes, then transfer to wire racks to cool completely.

Store in an airtight container and eat within 5 days or freeze for up to a month.

Variation Remove the dough from the processor and work in 75 g pecan pieces, then shape and bake the cookies as above.

Just a few drops of Tabasco sauce gives these moist and rich cookies a fascinating, subtle flavour. Ask your friends if they can guess the mystery ingredient.

macadamia and white choc chilli cookies

150 g macadamia nuts

200 g plain flour

½ teaspoon baking powder

100 g light muscovado sugar

115 g unsalted butter, very soft

1 large egg, lightly beaten

5 drops Tabasco sauce

100 g white chocolate, broken into chunks, or chips

several baking trays, greased

Makes 20

Put the nuts in an ovenproof dish and toast in a preheated oven at 180°C (350°F) Gas 4 for 5–7 minutes until light golden brown. Let cool, then chop coarsely by hand or in a food processor. Leave the oven on.

Put the chopped nuts, flour, baking powder, sugar, butter, egg, Tabasco and chocolate pieces in a large bowl and mix thoroughly with a wooden spoon.

Using about a tablespoon of the mixture for each cookie, drop each spoonful onto the prepared baking trays, spacing well apart.

Bake in the heated oven for 12–15 minutes until light golden brown.

Let cool on the trays for 2 minutes, then transfer to a wire rack to cool completely.

Store in an airtight container and eat within 4 days or freeze for up to a month.

These dark, dark chocolate cookies have a white 'crazy-paving' top. The effect is created by rolling the cookies in icing sugar just before baking. The surface then cracks to form the 'paving'.

chocolate crackle cookies

100 g plain chocolate, broken up

115 g unsalted butter, diced

175 g light muscovado sugar

1 large egg, beaten

2–3 drops real vanilla essence

175 g self-raising flour

½ teaspoon bicarbonate of soda

2 tablespoons icing sugar

several baking trays, greased

Makes 24

Put the chocolate, butter and sugar in a heatproof bowl and set over a saucepan of gently steaming water. Melt gently, stirring occasionally until smooth.

Remove the bowl from the pan and let cool for a minute. Stir in the egg, vanilla, flour and bicarbonate of soda and mix well.

Cover the bowl and chill until firm, about 20 minutes.

Put the icing sugar in a shallow dish. Using your hands, roll the dough into walnut-sized balls, then roll in the icing sugar to coat thoroughly. Set the balls on the prepared trays, spacing them well apart. Bake in a preheated oven at 200°C (400°F) Gas 6 for 10–12 minutes until just set.

Let cool on the tray for 2 minutes, then transfer to a wire rack to cool completely.

Store in an airtight container and eat within 5 days or freeze for up to a month.

celebration

These unusual cookies, made with the same rich ingredients used for a traditional British Christmas cake, come from Williamsburg, New England.

For speed, use a bag of mixed dried fruit (raisins, sultanas and currants) or the 'luxury' type, which includes cherries, and a ready-chopped mix of nuts like Brazils, walnuts, almonds and hazelnuts.

christmas cake cookies

225 g self-raising flour

⅛ teaspoon grated nutmeg

½ teaspoon mixed spice

110 g dark muscovado sugar

110 g unsalted butter, chilled and diced

2 large eggs, beaten

2 tablespoons sweet sherry, brandy or milk

100 g chopped mixed nuts

150 g mixed dried fruit (raisins, sultanas, currants)

Demerara sugar, for sprinkling

several baking trays, greased

Makes 20

Sieve the flour, nutmeg and mixed spice into a large bowl. Stir in the sugar. Add the pieces of butter and rub into the flour using the tips of your fingers until the mixture looks like coarse crumbs. You can also cut the butter into the flour using a knife or special pastry cutter. Add the eggs, sherry, nuts and dried fruit to the bowl and mix thoroughly with a wooden spoon.

Drop tablespoons of the mixture onto the prepared trays, spacing them well apart. Flatten them slightly with the back of a fork and sprinkle lightly with Demerara sugar.

Bake in a preheated oven at 180°C (350°F) Gas 4 for 12–15 minutes, until golden brown.

Let cool for 2 minutes to firm up, then transfer to a cooling rack to cool completely.

Store in an airtight container and eat within 5 days, or freeze for up to a month.

Pecans, grown in a belt that runs across the US southern states, are by far the most important and most popular nuts in North America, and were particularly prized by Algonquin Indians, who gave them their name *paccan*. In the South, pecans are used to enrich stuffings, breads, cakes, salads and cookies, as well as baked in pies. I found these rich and crumbly cookies on a visit to New Mexico.

santa fe wedding cookies

130 g plain flour

4 tablespoons light muscovado sugar

100 g unsalted butter, very soft

½ teaspoon vanilla essence

50 g pecan pieces, coarsely chopped

20 pecan halves, to decorate

icing sugar, to dust

several baking trays, greased

Makes 20

Put the flour, sugar, soft butter, vanilla and pecans in a bowl. Using a wooden spoon, work the ingredients until they come together to form a soft dough.

Using your hands, lightly floured, roll the mixture into 20 walnut-sized balls. Arrange them slightly apart on the prepared baking trays, then gently press a pecan half on top of each cookie. Bake in a preheated oven at 180°C (350°F) Gas 4 for 10–12 minutes until a light golden colour with slightly brown edges.

Remove from the oven, let cool on the trays for 2 minutes, then transfer to a wire rack to cool completely. Dust with plenty of icing sugar before serving. Handle carefully – these cookies are fragile.

Store in an airtight container and eat within 5 days, or freeze for up to a month.

I've adapted a very old recipe that became famous because it was written by Sinclair Lewis, the Nobel and Pulitzer prize-winning author of *Elmer Gantry*. The bourbon adds an exotic and festive tang.

sinclair lewis's christmas cookies

110 g unsalted butter, very soft

150 g caster sugar

1 large egg, lightly beaten

150 g plain flour

a pinch of salt

3 tablespoons of cocoa powder

1 tablespoon bourbon or milk

40 g almonds, sliced, slivered, shredded, chopped or flaked

several baking trays, greased

Makes about 24

Put the soft butter and sugar in a bowl and beat with an electric whisk or mixer, or a wooden spoon, until creamy. Gradually beat in the egg.

Sift the flour, salt and cocoa into the bowl. Add the bourbon and almonds and mix well with a wooden spoon.

Using a heaped teaspoon of mixture for each cookie, spoon the mixture in mounds onto the prepared trays, spacing well apart.

Bake in a preheated oven at 160°C (325°F) Gas 3 for 10–12 minutes, until firm but not coloured.

Let cool on the trays for 2 minutes, then transfer to a wire rack to cool completely.

Store in an airtight container and eat within 4 days or freeze for up to a month.

Make edible Christmas decorations by cutting the spicy shortbread-like dough into tree, star or bell shapes. After baking, decorate with ready-made icing pens and silver balls and thread with ribbons for hanging.

german honey spice cookies

150 g plain flour

1 teaspoon ground cinnamon

¼ teaspoon ground ginger

¼ teaspoon ground mixed spice

85 g unsalted butter, chilled and diced

3 tablespoons clear honey

To finish (optional)

thin ribbon, for hanging

edible icing writing pens

silver balls

shaped biscuit cutters

several baking trays, greased

Makes about 12 (depending on size)

Put the flour, cinnamon, ginger and mixed spice in a food processor. Add the butter and blend until the mixture looks like crumbs. Add the honey and process until it comes together to make a soft dough.

Remove the dough from the processor, wrap in clingfilm or greaseproof paper and chill for 30 minutes or until firm.

Lightly flour the work surface and a rolling pin, then roll out the dough to about 5 mm thick. Cut out shapes using biscuit cutters. If making as Christmas decorations, use a cocktail stick to pierce a hole at the top of each shape large enough to thread a thin ribbon through it.

Arrange the shapes slightly apart on the prepared trays and chill for 10 minutes. Bake in a preheated oven at 180°C (350°F) Gas 4 for about 10 minutes until golden. Let cool for 5 minutes, then transfer to a wire rack to cool completely.

When cold, leave plain or thread with ribbon, decorate with ready-made icing (in writing pens) and silver balls, leave until set, then hang them up.

Best eaten within 24 hours if used as decorations, or store in an airtight container and eat within 4 days. Undecorated cookies can be frozen for up to a month.

Brigitte, a friend from Berlin, always makes these attractive sticky squares to celebrate the first Sunday in Advent (to mark the four weeks before Christmas).

honey and almond squares

175 g plain flour

115 g unsalted butter, chilled and diced

2 tablespoons caster sugar

1 egg yolk

½ teaspoon vanilla essence

Topping

175 g flaked almonds

85 g unsalted butter

3 tablespoons caster sugar

2 tablespoons set honey

2 tablespoons cream (single or double)

a Swiss roll tin or shallow baking tin about 30 x 20 cm, greased

Makes 32

To make the base, put the flour, diced butter, sugar, egg yolk and vanilla essence in a food processor. Blend until the mixture just comes together to make a smooth, firm dough. The ingredients can also be put in a mixing bowl and worked together by hand.

Transfer the dough to the prepared tin and press over the base of the tin with floured fingers to make an even layer. Prick the dough base all over with a fork, then chill for 10 minutes. Meanwhile, preheat the oven to 190°C (375°F) Gas 5.

Bake the dough base in the heated oven for 10–12 minutes until firm and golden. Remove from the oven (don't turn the oven off) and let cool while making the topping.

To make the topping, put the almonds, butter, sugar and honey in a non-stick frying pan, or wide, heavy saucepan. Cook over low heat, stirring constantly with a wooden spoon, until a pale straw colour. Stir in the cream and cook for 10 seconds. Remove the pan from the heat and pour the mixture over the cooked base. Spread evenly, then bake for 10 minutes until a good golden colour.

Let cool in the tin, then cut into small squares. Store in an airtight container and eat within 5 days. Not suitable for freezing.

This recipe for snowy-white, rich almond cookies comes from a Czech friend, but I've eaten Polish, German and Dutch versions, and my mother-in-law makes something similar during Hannukah.

czech almond crescents

125 g whole blanched almonds

60 g icing sugar, plus extra for dusting

115 g unsalted butter, chilled and diced

2–3 drops real almond essence

100 g plain flour

several baking trays, well greased

Makes 24

Put the almonds and sugar in a food processor and blend until the mixture becomes a fine, sandy powder.

Add the butter, almond essence and flour and process until the mixture forms a ball of smooth dough.

Carefully remove the dough from the machine, wrap in clingfilm and chill for about 20 minutes or until firm. The dough can be stored in the refrigerator for 24 hours.

When ready to finish, preheat the oven to 160°C (325°F) Gas 3. Take a heaped teaspoon of dough and roll it with your hands to make a sausage shape about 7 cm long. Curve the dough into a crescent and set on a prepared baking tray. Repeat with the rest of the dough, arranging the crescents well apart on the trays.

Bake in the heated oven for 15–18 minutes until the edges are barely coloured. Let cool on the trays for 2 minutes, then carefully transfer to a wire rack to cool completely. Just before serving, dust with plenty of icing sugar.

Store in an airtight container and eat within a week. These cookies are fragile and, while they can be frozen, they tend to break easily.

Variation Gently melt 50 g good quality plain chocolate and dip one end of each cooled cookie into the chocolate. Let set on non-stick baking parchment. Sprinkle the plain end with icing sugar before serving.

Rich, traditional and crumbly, these biscuits were made to contrast with the privations of Lent, and echo the rich (and expensive) flavours of simnel cakes – dried fruit, butter and spices or lemon.

west country easter biscuits

115 g unsalted butter, very soft

80 g golden caster sugar

1 egg yolk

the finely grated zest of 1 unwaxed lemon

200 g plain flour

a good pinch of baking powder

a pinch of salt

50 g sultanas

Topping

1 egg white, lightly beaten

golden caster sugar, for sprinkling

a fluted biscuit cutter, 7 cm diameter

several baking trays, greased

Makes 16

Put the soft butter, sugar and egg yolk in a bowl and beat with a wooden spoon, electric mixer or whisk, until light and creamy. Beat in the lemon zest, then add the flour, baking powder, salt and sultanas. Mix with a wooden spoon. Bring the dough together with your hands. Wrap and chill until firm – about 20 minutes. At this point, the dough can be stored in the refrigerator for up to 3 days.

Roll out the dough on a floured work surface to about 5 mm thick. Cut into rounds with the fluted biscuit cutter. Arrange well apart on the prepared baking trays.

Bake in a preheated oven at 200°C (400°F) Gas 6 for about 10 minutes until pale golden and firm.

Remove the trays from the oven and lightly brush each biscuit with beaten egg white, then sprinkle with a little sugar. Return to the oven and bake for a further 3–5 minutes or until the tops have become golden and crunchy.

Remove from the oven and let cool on the tray for a minute, then transfer to a wire rack to cool completely.

Store in an airtight container and eat within 5 days or freeze for up to a month.

Variation Omit the lemon zest. Add ½ teaspoon ground mixed spice, ½ teaspoon ground cinnamon and a good pinch of grated nutmeg to the flour. Use currants or raisins instead of the sultanas, and add 1 teaspoon finely chopped mixed candied peel if you like.

These sweet, almond-rich cookies are like soft, chewy amaretti. Serve with coffee at the end a special meal; a box of them makes a lovely gift.

sardinian wedding cookies

450 g almond paste

70 g flaked almonds

2 medium egg whites

50 g icing sugar

30 g flaked almonds

several baking trays lined with non-stick baking parchment

Makes 30

Break up the almond paste and put in a food processor. Process briefly until the paste is finely chopped. Add the almonds, egg whites and sugar and process until the mixture forms a thick, smooth paste.

Using a tablespoon of mixture for each cookie, drop or spoon the mixture onto the prepared trays, spacing the cookies slightly apart. Scatter the remaining almonds over the top of the cookies.

Bake in a preheated oven at 150°C (300°F) Gas 2 for about 25 minutes until light golden brown. Let cool completely on the trays, then remove the cookies. Store in an airtight container and eat within a week. These cookies don't freeze very well.

Variation Replace the almonds (in the mixture and for sprinkling) with pine nuts.

Traditionally made for the Christmas holidays, these dark spicy cookies can be left plain or decorated with white icing – you can use ready-made icing writing pens for this.

swedish pepper cookies

200 g plain flour

½ teaspoon bicarbonate of soda

1 teaspoon ground cinnamon

1 teaspoon ground ginger

½ teaspoon ground black pepper

the freshly grated zest of 1 unwaxed orange

150 g caster sugar

115 g unsalted butter, chilled and diced

1 medium egg, lightly beaten

1 tablespoon black treacle

star-shaped biscuit cutter

several baking trays, greased

Makes about 15

Put all the ingredients in a food processor and blend until the mixture forms a soft dough.

Remove the dough from the processor, wrap in clingfilm or greaseproof paper and chill for 1 hour or until firm.

Lightly flour the work surface and a rolling pin and roll out the dough to about 5 mm thick. Stamp out star shapes with the biscuit cutter.

Arrange the shapes slightly apart on the prepared trays and chill for 10 minutes.

Bake in a preheated oven at 160°C (325°F) Gas 3 for 10–12 minutes until dark golden brown and firm.

Let cool for 5 minutes, then transfer to a wire rack and let cool completely. Add decoration, if using (see recipe introduction). Store in an airtight container and eat within a week or freeze undecorated cookies for up to a month.

savoury

Truly rich and crumbly, these savoury biscuits are hard to resist, and they rapidly disappear at parties. The cheese dough can be kept in the refrigerator for a week before baking, making for easy entertaining.

walnut cheddar shortbreads

130 g plain flour

115 g unsalted butter, chilled and diced

115 g mature Cheddar cheese, grated

3 pinches of ground black pepper or cayenne

3 tablespoons walnut pieces

several baking trays, lightly greased

Makes 25

Put the flour, diced butter, grated cheese and pepper in a food processor. Process just until the mixture looks like very coarse crumbs, then add the walnut pieces. Process again briefly, until the mixture forms a very soft dough. Remove the dough from the processor, put onto a piece of clingfilm or greaseproof paper and shape into a brick about 12 x 4 x 6 cm.

Wrap and chill until firm, about an hour. The dough can be kept in the refrigerator, well wrapped, for up to a week.

Using a large, sharp knife, slice the dough very thinly, about 3 mm.

Arrange the slices slightly apart on the prepared baking trays and bake in a preheated oven at 180°C (350°F) Gas 4 for about 12 minutes until the edges turn light brown. Let cool on the trays for a minute, then transfer to a wire rack to cool completely.

Store in an airtight container (these biscuits are fragile) and eat within 3 days or freeze for up to a month.

Pronounced 'poacha', these cheese-filled savoury sesame biscuits are a favourite with my Turkish friend Zeynep. Use feta cheese, ready diced and marinated in oil and herbs or peppers, or another feta or similar cheese. Eat warm with soup or with drinks.

pogaca

250 g self-raising flour

½ teaspoon sea salt

2 good pinches of dried chilli flakes

½ teaspoon bicarbonate of soda

125 ml olive oil

125 ml plain yoghurt

90 g feta cheese (drained weight), cut into 30 small pieces

1 egg yolk, beaten, to glaze

sesame seeds, for sprinkling

several baking trays, greased

Makes 30

Put the flour, salt, chilli flakes, bicarbonate of soda, oil and yoghurt in a food processor and blend until the mixture comes together to form a ball of soft but not sticky dough. Remove the dough from the processor, wrap in clingfilm or greaseproof paper and chill for 1 hour.

Flour your fingers, then take about a heaped teaspoon of dough, roll it into a ball with your hands, then press it out to a thin disc about 6 cm across. Put a cube of feta in the centre, then fold the disc in half to make a half-moon shape. Press the edges together – don't worry if it is not neat. Repeat with the rest of the dough. Put the pogaca on the prepared baking trays, spacing slightly apart.

Brush the tops with beaten egg yolk, sprinkle with plenty of sesame seeds, then bake in a preheated oven at 180°C (350°F) Gas 4 for 12–15 minutes until light golden brown.

Cool on the trays for a minute, then eat warm from the oven, or transfer to a wire cooling rack to cool completely.

Store in an airtight container in the refrigerator and eat within 24 hours, or freeze for up to a month. Warm gently before serving.

Though designed to eat with soft cheeses, particularly goats' cheese, and strong, hard cheeses such as Stilton and Cheddar, these are also good with soups.

wheaten biscuits

170 g plain wholemeal flour

½ teaspoon sea salt

½ teaspoon baking powder

50 g porridge oats or rolled oats

1½ tablespoons caster sugar

100 g unsalted butter, chilled and diced

½ teaspoon garam masala

1 large egg, lightly beaten

a biscuit cutter, about 6.5 cm diameter

several baking trays, greased

Makes about 20

Put the flour, salt, baking powder, oats, sugar, butter, and garam masala in a food processor. Blend for a few seconds until the mixture looks like coarse breadcrumbs. Add the beaten egg and process until the mixture comes together to make a firm dough.

Remove the dough from the processor, put onto a floured work surface and roll out to about 5 mm thick. Cut out rounds with the biscuit cutter. Knead the trimmings together, then re-roll and cut out more rounds.

Arrange the biscuits slightly apart on the prepared trays, prick with a fork and bake in a preheated oven at 190°C (375°F) Gas 5 for 12–15 minutes until slightly brown around the edges.

Let cool on the trays for 2 minutes, then transfer to a wire rack to cool completely.

Store in an airtight container and eat within a week or freeze for up to a month.

Variation To make Sweet Wheaten Biscuits, omit the garam masala and increase the sugar to 45 g.

It's hard to eat just one of these crisp, savoury crackers, so they're perfect with drinks at party time, or with a bowl of soup. The recipe comes from Alyson Cook, who caters to the stars of Hollywood.

alyson's parmesan herb crisps

85 g Parmigiano Reggiano cheese, freshly grated

130 g plain flour

110 g unsalted butter, chilled and diced

½ teaspoon dried herbes de Provence

½ teaspoon Worcestershire sauce

2 tablespoons white wine (optional)

non-stick baking parchment

several baking trays, greased

Makes 50–60

Put all the ingredients in a food processor and blend until the mixture forms a ball of dough.

Remove the dough from the processor and put on a sheet of non-stick baking parchment. Shape into a log about 30 x 2.5 cm.

Wrap tightly, then chill until firm, about 2 hours. The mixture can be kept in the refrigerator for up to 4 days.

When ready to cook, preheat the oven to 190°C (375°F) Gas 5. Cut the log into 5 mm slices.

Arrange the slices well apart on the prepared baking trays and bake in the heated oven for 12–15 minutes until light golden brown.

Let cool on the trays for 2 minutes, then transfer to a wire rack to cool completely. Store in an airtight container and eat within 5 days or freeze for up to a month.

Crisp, crumbly Scottish oatcakes have been made for centuries and are still very popular. They are good with soft cheeses or strong Cheddars, or spread with butter and jam or honey. This recipe uses olive oil rather than the traditional lard, as well as fine oatmeal, available from wholefood stores.

oatcakes

220 g fine oatmeal, plus extra for rolling out

½ teaspoon sea salt

2 pinches of baking powder

3 tablespoons olive oil

100 ml boiling water

a round biscuit cutter, about 6.5 cm diameter

several baking trays, greased

Makes about 16

Put the oatmeal, salt, baking powder and olive oil in a food processor. With the motor running, pour in the boiling water through the feed tube. Process until the mixture just comes together. Remove the dough from the processor and put onto a work surface sprinkled with oatmeal. If the dough is very sticky, work in a little extra oatmeal – the dough soon firms up.

Roll out the dough to about 4 mm thick, then cut out rounds using the biscuit cutter. Knead the trimmings together, then re-roll and cut out more rounds.

Arrange the oatcakes slightly apart on the prepared trays and bake in a preheated oven at 160°C (325°F) Gas 3 for about 15 minutes until the edges are lightly browned.

Let cool on the trays for 2 minutes, then transfer to a wire rack to cool completely.

Store in an airtight container and eat within a week or freeze for up to a month.

If the oatcakes become soft, they can be crisped up in the oven (heated as above) for 5 minutes.

Variations At the same time as the oatmeal, add either:
• 3 pinches of chilli flakes to make Spicy Oatcakes
• 4 teaspoons poppy seeds or sesame seeds
• 1 tablespoon fresh thyme leaves.

index